Jesus said, "Let the little children come to Me, and do not
hinder them, for the kingdom of God belongs to such as
these." (Matthew 19:14 and Mark 10:14)

    The FamilyTime Bible Stories series is dedicated to
Jesus, and to families. It is the hope and prayer of those who
worked on these stories that they would help families grow
closer to God.

    To my own family, Erik, Julia and Daniel.

                    Anne de Graaf
                    August 1987

Book 6

Soldiers of the Lord

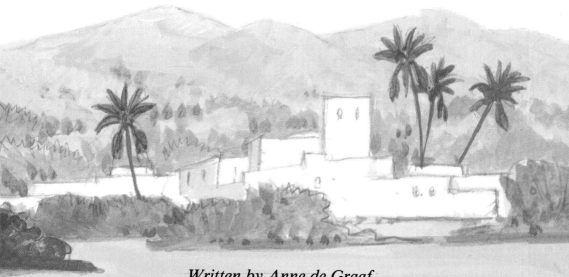

Written by Anne de Graaf
Illustrated by José Pérez Montero.

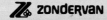

ZONDERVAN

FamilyTime Bible Stories

Canaan – Soldiers of the Lord

Table of Contents — Joshua 5-end; Judges

Introduction to the Book of Judges

The Book of Judges tells about the time after the Israelites settled in Canaan. There, they grew stronger and stronger. Although there were many who forgot to follow God's laws, there were also a few who continued in the way God had set before them. The people of Israel had no king. From time to time, God gave them a wise man or woman who told them over and over again, they must follow God. These were the judges.

In the years after Joshua's death Israel became a nation of scattered tribes. People from one tribe did not often see people from the other. Each tribe lived its own life, with the people raising sheep, growing crops and living from day to day. Because there was no one leader like Moses or Joshua to bind the people together, they often chose to forget or ignore the laws God had given them to follow.

As time passed, the people of Israel became more and more like the enemy tribes living around them. They worshipped other gods and lived evil lives. Whenever they did not do what God had told them, God allowed the Canaanite tribes to attack Israel and win. Then the people would cry out for help from God.

No matter how many times the people were bad, whenever they said they were sorry and asked God for His help, He listened. Time and time again He sent judges who could help lead the Israelites back to lives which honored God.

They decided who was right and wrong and taught the people wisdom. They also reminded God's people of the laws they should be following. The judges trusted God and believed in His love. That was all God needed in order to make them into leaders. Unfortunately, every time a judge would die, the people forgot and went back to their evil ways.

GOD KEEPS HIS PROMISES

The Israelites Start Over

Joshua 5:1-:2

The Israelites made camp on the Canaan side of the river. It was their first night in the new land. They were excited and tired. The men were especially excited because they knew soon Joshua would lead them in battle against other tribes. This time, the land they won would be their own.

During the next few days all Joshua's soldiers sharpened their swords and spears. They were ready to take the city of Jericho. But Joshua had other plans.

He called the leaders of the twelve Israelite families to him.

"Maybe we will get our battle orders," they said to each other.

"Men, before we do anything else, we must show that we are a people set apart by God," Joshua said. "When our fathers lived in Egypt and ever since Abraham was chosen by God, the men of Israel marked their bodies to show they belonged to God."

The men nodded. Yes, it was true. But none of them had had this done because they had all been born out in the wilderness, during the long journey of the last forty years.

"Now that we are in the promised land, it is time to show again that we belong to God. So now all the men and boys will have to have their bodies marked in this special way. This shows we are God's people and that we promise to keep His laws."

The men were amazed because Joshua had chosen what they thought was one of the worst times for doing this. Why, there were enemy tribes all around them. The men would be sore for several days as they waited for the marks to heal. They could not fight then.

"What if we are attacked?" they wondered.

God's Agreement

Joshua 5:3-:12

Despite their doubts, the men followed Joshua's orders. During the next few days every man and boy in the Israelite camp was marked.

In doing this, the people showed they wanted to start over with God. The long trip in the wilderness was finished. Now they wanted to keep their promises.

God had made a deal long ago. The deal said all of Abraham's family would show they belonged to God. If they did this and tried their hardest to do what God said, God would give them the promised land.

Although the Israelites were already in the land, Joshua knew it would still take many wars before the land was theirs. He wanted God to know they trusted Him.

Every day of their journey through the wilderness the people had trusted God to feed them. He always sent the manna bread and they never went hungry. But once the Israelites crossed the River Jordan, God stopped sending manna bread. They did not need it anymore because they could live off the fruit and grain which grew in the land. The people were not forced to trust God as they had been in the desert.

But they did have to trust God to protect them while they were weak. And God did. None of the nearby tribes attacked them. All their enemies had heard how the River Jordan had split in half and become dry just for the Israelites. They were very, very scared. They knew God was on the side of Joshua and his soldiers. None of the enemy tribes dared attack Israel.

A Plan to Capture Jericho

Joshua 5:13-6:11

Joshua waited until all the Israelite men were feeling better. He waited until they were strong again. He waited until God told him it was time. Then Joshua ordered his soldiers to capture the city of Jericho.

Joshua called for the two men who had spied on the city. They told Joshua all about where the guards were and how rich the king of Jericho was. "But we must not harm the prostitute Rahab," they said. "She believes in the one God and helped us escape." Joshua agreed.

Then Joshua fell on his knees and prayed for the Lord to help them capture Jericho. God gave Joshua a very strange plan. It was not at all the normal way to fight a battle.

He told his captains, "We will have a parade."

None of Joshua's soldiers had ever fought like that before. A parade was not a battle! But they listened to the plan from God as Joshua told them.

"Yes," they said, "we will try that. We will do what God says."

The next day all the soldiers lined up. It did indeed look like a parade. First the priests carried the ark. Then came Joshua, leading all the soldiers.

When the people in the city of Jericho saw the Israelites coming, they shook with fear. "Oh," they cried, "this will be a terrible battle and we shall all die because God is on their side."

But the Israelites surprised them. They did not attack. Instead, they lined up and walked around the city. They marched the whole way around the walls which surrounded the city. And as they marched, the soldiers were very quiet. Joshua had told them not to make a sound. There were no battle cries, no yells or shouts, just hundreds and hundreds of quiet soldiers. The only sound was that of seven priests, playing on their trumpets.

The Battle Won with Trumpets

Joshua 6:12-:27

When the people of Jericho heard the trumpet music, they said, "Why are they doing this, it only makes us more afraid!"

After the Israelites had marched around Jericho, they went back to their camp and rested.

The next day they did the same thing. All the soldiers lined up and followed the priests who carried the ark and played the trumpets. They went around the city once, then went home.

The next day and the next, for six days they paraded around Jericho. All the while, they made no sound except for the trumpets.

Then, on the seventh day, Joshua ordered his army to walk around Jericho seven times, instead of once. And on the seventh time, when the trumpets blew, the soldiers let out a great whoop, they yelled as loud as they could.

"Boom! Crash!" No sooner had the soldiers yelled when the very walls of Jericho fell in. All that stone tumbled down into great heaps. God had worked another miracle and the Israelite soldiers did not even have to fight or climb the tall walls. God brought the walls down for them.

The Israelites poured into the city and they killed all the people and burned their houses to the ground. God had told them not to take any of the gold or silver, though, since that would be

for God's own treasure chests which the priests took care of. All the people of Jericho were killed that day, except for one woman and her family.

That woman was Rahab. One of the spies had found her house after the walls fell in. The red cord was swinging from a window. He told her to hurry and bring her parents and family. Then he brought her to a safe place outside the city.

When the battle was over Rahab said she wanted to join the Israelites. They welcomed her. She believed in the one, true God and had been very brave. She became one of them. Many, many years later, Rahab would become the great-great-grandmother of the mighty King David of Israel.

7

THE UNBEATABLE ARMY

The Sun Listened

Joshua 10:1-:43

Up and down and all around Canaan Joshua led
his mighty army. No matter how great the
soldiers were from the other tribes, the Israelites
always defeated them. Everywhere they went,
they won. It was just a matter of time before the
whole land was theirs.

There were five kings who knew the Israelites
would soon attack their cities. They held a secret
meeting and tried to come up with a plan. They
agreed they would add all their armies together,
then instead of five little armies they would have
one very big army. And maybe, just maybe, the
army would be big enough to overcome the
Israelites.

Their army may have been big enough to beat
the Israelites, but it was not big enough to beat
God. God is bigger than every army in the world
put together.

God told Joshua when he should attack the
army of the five kings. He surprised them at
night and soon all five kings, together with their
armies, were running for their lives.

God wanted to help the Israelites even more.
So He sent big, gray clouds. The sky grew very
dark. There was thunder and lightning! Instead
of rain falling from the dark clouds, huge
hailstones tumbled out of the sky. The hail fell
onto the enemy soldiers' heads and many, many
were killed. There were more soldiers killed by
God's hailstones than by the spears of the
Israelites.

Then Joshua called out in a loud voice to the
Lord, "O sun, stand still, o moon, stand still!"
The Lord did as Joshua asked. He made the sun
and moon stand still. There was a long, long,
dark day. And the enemies of Israel thought the
terrible day would never end.

The day did not end until all five kings had
been captured in a cave and their armies chased
away or killed. Once again, the Israelites had
won because God was on their side.

The Land Is Conquered and Divided

Joshua 11:1-:23, 13:1-22:34; Numbers 34:1-35:33

The Israelites fought war after war, battle after battle. Time and time again they won. Because God was helping them, giving them wisdom and courage, they always won. Slowly but surely, the land of Canaan fell into their hands.

More kings banded together, hoping to make an army so big and powerful the Israelites would have to lose. But the Lord helped His chosen people and once again they defeated their enemy. The Israelites always won, no matter how big or small their enemy was.

Finally, there came a time when most of the land which God had promised the Israelites belonged to them. "It is time to rest," the great General Joshua said to his people. After so many years of wandering in the desert and so many years of fighting wars, the Israelites were ready for peace.

They wanted to plant their fields and work at making their crops grow. They wanted to take care of their animals and have time to play with their children. It was time to settle the land of Canaan.

Joshua called a huge conference of all the people. The twelve leaders of the twelve tribes of Israel lined up in front of him. He drew a map of Canaan and divided it into twelve parts, including the parts on the other side of the River Jordan. Then he gave to each tribe their part of the land. That would be where they could plant their crops, build homes, pasture their sheep. Now all the people had homes. Before they set off, Joshua made them promise again to follow the laws of God.

The tribes who settled on the other side of the Jordan built a big altar. When the other tribes of Israel saw that, they thought those tribes were worshipping the wrong gods.

"But it is not true!" the tribes said. "This altar we have built is to show we are one family. Someday you on that side of the Jordan River might decide we are no longer your family because we live so far away. But this altar will remind you of the truth. We are all members of God's chosen people. Let there always be peace between us."

The tribes agreed.

Joshua's Parting Words

Joshua 23:1-24:33

God gave the people of Israel many years of peace in their new homes. They settled in villages, lived in cities they had taken away from

enemies, ate the harvest from their crops and lived happily.

Several years passed. Joshua was the great general of Moses, the man who led the Israelites across the River Jordan. The soldier for the Lord who had beat army after army of enemy tribes had grown into an old man. He was 110 years old and he knew soon he would die. He called all the leaders of the people together.

He read to them from God's law and he asked the people if they would obey God.

"Yes, we will serve the Lord!" they yelled back.

"But you will not serve Him!" Joshua answered. "You are a naughty people who are always forgetting what you promise. You will probably go off and worship some worthless god!"

"No! No!" the cried. "Why should we do that when it was God who brought us out of Egypt and gave us this land? No, we will worship and serve God!"

Then Joshua made all the people promise never, ever to worship any of the gods which the other tribes around them worshipped. This was why God told Moses the enemy tribes must all be killed. He knew if the people saw other tribes worshipping other gods, they would want to as well.

Joshua warned them, "The same God Almighty who has kept all His promises and given you all this land, can destroy you if you make Him angry by worshipping other gods. Remember that!"

Then he passed on the message Moses had said to him, when he died. "Be brave, remember the Lord always and be brave!"

The bravest soldier of them all, Joshua, God's general for the Israelites, died. His people buried him and were sad for a long, long time.

Joshua had not chosen any one man to be the leader over the people. Instead, they were each supposed to follow the Lord as their leader. The next years would be a time of testing for the Israelites.

A TIME WHEN WISDOM IS NEEDED

God's Messenger Speaks to Troubled Israel

Judges 1:1-3:6

Many, many years passed. Because Egypt and the mighty battles led by Joshua had happened so long ago, the children of the people who left Egypt did not believe the stories. The tale of God bringing the Israelites out of slavery never became anything more than just that, a tale.

"Why should we follow a lot of rules?" they asked each other.

"Who cares about a God none of us has ever met? Maybe all that religion was all right for our parents," they said, "but we want something else."

At first, God continued helping them win battles against the enemy Canaanite tribes. But as the Israelites kept on choosing to forget they were a chosen people, God no longer helped them. They lost wars. And when they lost, they had to sign treaties with their enemies.

One day, the leaders of Israel had a visitor. The men looked up and saw a tall, shining angel standing at the door. They fell onto the ground in fear.

"Have you forgotten that God brought you out of Egypt?" the angel asked. "Have you forgotten that you are a special nation set apart by God? God told you not to sign treaties with the enemies. You have not won your battles because you forgot the stories your parents told you. You forgot they were not just stories, but the laws of God. Because you did not obey, you lost. And now you have disobeyed again by making peace with the very people God wanted you to destroy."

The people were shaking. They realized they had been very bad. What should they do?

The angel said, "God will not help you defeat these enemies. You must live next to them and year after year, they will make life hard because you will be tempted to live as they do, rather than as the Lord has commanded. These people will test you forever."

When the angel left, the leaders thought, "Yes, we have been wrong." So the people all made offerings and prayed to God, promising to do better.

It did not take long until they forgot again, though. They married the daughters of the Canaanite tribes, something God had said not to do. They lived bad lives and worst of all, they worshipped other gods. God was very angry with His people.

The Wise Woman under the Palm Tree

Judges 4:1-:16

Because the Israelites worshipped other gods, the Lord allowed an enemy, King Jabin and his General Sisera, to conquer the Israelites. King Jabin was very cruel. But God let King Jabin take over the land because He wanted His people to learn they would only have peace if they followed God.

The Lord sent a woman named Deborah to judge over Israel then. God had blessed her with wisdom and she loved the Lord God very much. She often reminded her people to listen to God and obey Him, but most of them just laughed at her.

As a judge, Deborah held court and listened to all the problems of the people. When Deborah held court, she sat underneath a big palm tree. Then all the people stood in line, waiting to talk to her.

One day Deborah sent for Barak, an Israelite soldier. "Barak, you are to take ten thousand men and lead the way to Mount Tabor. When General Sisera hears you are there, he will bring his chariots and troops and then we will defeat him at the river."

Barak lowered his head in shame. "I cannot do this," he said. "I cannot lead ten thousand men into a battle where they are doomed to die."

"No," Deborah said softly. "They will not die. God will help us win."

"Well, all right. If you say so, Deborah, it must be true. But I tell you, I will not fight this battle unless you are there, too."

Deborah smiled at him. "Is your faith in God less than your faith in me?" she asked. "Yes, I will be there with you. But because you did not trust God, He will give the credit for the victory to a woman instead of to you."

He nodded and walked back home. He wondered where he would ever find ten thousand Israelite men to fight Sisera and his iron chariots.

Soon the day of the battle came. Barak and Deborah led the ten thousand Israelites to the top of Mount Tabor and waited. Soon Sisera gathered together his nine hundred iron chariots and all his troops and brought them to the river.

Deborah said, "Go, Barak! Go! On this day the Lord will make you win! God is with you!"

While Barak led his troops and Deborah prayed on the mountaintop, God caused all sorts of things to go wrong within Sisera's troops. The worst was when rain poured into the river, causing it to flood. The brave soldiers of Sisera suddenly felt afraid. This was certainly not like any battle they had ever fought before.

And before Barak knew it, he was chasing all Sisera's soldiers into the hills. The Israelites had won!

Who Will Kill Sisera?

Judges 4:17-:22, 5:1-:31

When General Sisera saw he had lost the battle against the Israelites, he ran away into the hills, hoping to find a place to hide. He spotted the home of one of King Jabin's friends. "Ah," he thought, "these people are on our side."

A woman came out to meet him. Her name was Jael. "Come, my lord, come right in. Don't be afraid," she said. Sisera entered. He could not know, but secretly, Jael wanted Sisera and his army to lose. Jael gave him some milk, then covered him with a blanket.

When General Sisera fell sound asleep, Jael snuck over to his side. She carried a tent stake and hammer in her hands. Jael looked down at Sisera as he slept. He was an evil man who had hurt a lot of people. Using the stake, Jael killed General Sisera.

Meanwhile, Barak was looking for Sisera. As he came to Jael's tent, Jael went out to meet him.

"The man you are looking for is inside," she said. Barak went in and there lay General Sisera, dead on the floor of Jael's tent.

Barak brought Jael back to Deborah. Together the three returned to the palm tree. The Israelites cheered wildly. They called out, "Who killed Sisera?"

Barak looked at Deborah. Her prophecy had come true. The credit for Sisera's death must go to a woman. He held Jael's hand up high so the crowd could see her. "This woman! Jael killed Sisera!"

All the Israelites cheered Jael. Deborah and Barak reminded them, though, it was the Lord God who had won the war for them. They even sang a song about God's victory.

Barak and Deborah were judges over the Israelite people for the next forty years. During that time, many came to know the love of God and learn His laws. God blessed the people with peace as they listened to Him.

15

GIDEON'S FLEECE

Gideon Is Afraid

Judges 6:1-:23

The people were good while Barak and Deborah lived. But once they died, the people fell into their old ways again and forgot their promises. They worshipped other gods. They were mean. They did not say "thank you" to God for His blessings. Worst of all, they stopped trusting God and loving Him.

To teach and remind them they were His chosen people, God allowed the Midianite enemies to conquer the Israelites.

For seven years, the Israelites were the prisoners of the Midianites. The Midianites were fierce fighters. They rode their camels at breakneck speeds, running over anyone who got in their way.

Once again, though, the people finally remembered God when they had no food and suffered from the cruel Midianites. They called out to God. "Save us, please!"

God heard His people and sent a wise man, or judge, to help them. God chose Gideon.

Gideon was hiding in a cave, secretly grinding grain so his family would have something to eat. He did it as quietly and secretly as possible.

Gideon looked up from his work and saw a man sitting very close to him, under a nearby tree.

The stranger was an angel, but Gideon did not know that yet. The angel said, "The Lord is with you, mighty warrior."

"If the Lord is with us, sir," Gideon said, "why doesn't He save us from these horrible people, the Midianites? Our parents told us lovely stories about a God who cared, but I think they were just silly stories."

"No, Gideon, they were not just stories. Look, the Lord has chosen you to lead the Israelites and chase the Midianites out of Canaan."

At that, Gideon's heart nearly stopped. "Me?

How can the Lord choose me? I'm the weakest member of the weakest family of the weakest tribe. Why me? I'm nothing."

Gideon did not doubt God could work such a miracle. He had faith and that is why God chose him and not someone else. Also, because Gideon was weak, it would take that much more faith in God to trust in a victory. Still, Gideon had to be sure.

He prepared some meat, bread and soup, then brought it to the stranger. The angel reached out his staff and touched the meat. Fire flared from the rock, and the meat and bread disappeared, as did the angel.

Only then did Gideon realize to whom he had been talking. "Oh great Lord! I have been talking to an angel face to face!"

But the Lord said to him, "Peace! Do not be afraid. You are not going to die."

17

Gideon Begins His Work

Judges 6:24-:39

Gideon was so excited about seeing an angel, he built an altar at that very spot and made an offering. He thanked God for being so good to him. He even called the place, "The Lord Is Peace."

When it became dark, Gideon fell asleep. That night the Lord came to Gideon and said, "Gideon, go to the altar of the other gods. Tear down that altar and build a new one. The new altar will be for Me. Bring two bulls with you and offer them up to Me."

Gideon knew the other men in the village could kill him for tearing down the altar of their gods, but he did what God had asked of him.

There was no moon as he and ten of his servants snuck up the hill to the place where the foreign gods were worshipped. The wind sang through the treetops. An owl hooted.

Gideon tied up the two bulls to the stones and made them pull it all down. Quietly, very quietly, Gideon and his servants built a new altar. They killed one of the bulls and burned it on the altar, praying to God for protection.

God answered their prayers. The next morning when the men of the village discovered someone had destroyed the altar of their gods, they said, "Where is the one who did it? We will kill him!"

But Joash, Gideon's father said, "If your god is really a god, let him punish the culprit and you stay out of it." The men agreed. So Gideon was safe and the altar of the Lord remained.

Soon many enemy tribes banded together, including the terrible Midianites. They planned to kill all the Israelites. But the Holy Spirit of God, who makes people strong and wise, came upon Gideon. He felt brave and knew what he should do.

Gideon picked up his trumpet and blew a mighty blast. Then, just to make sure God was on his side, Gideon put God to the test. "Lord, if You are really going to help Israel win, then please show me. If I put this sheepskin on the ground for the night and it is wet with dew, and the ground around it is dry, then I will know we are doing what You want by going into battle."

And it was so. The next morning the sheepskin was dry, but the ground was wet. "Lord, forgive me, please. But may I test You yet one more time? Tonight, could You please make the ground wet with dew, but keep the sheepskin dry?"

And it was so. This way Gideon had no doubt at all that he was doing what God wanted.

It Takes Fewer Men to Win the Battle

Judges 7:1-:8

Many men followed Gideon. He spoke like a leader and they could tell God was blessing him. They all wanted to fight for Gideon and beat the Midianites. So Gideon led the people to a river. On the other side was the Midianite army.

But the Lord said, "Gideon, there are too many soldiers with you. If I let you fight and you win, the people might become proud and think they did it all by themselves. I want to teach them to lean on Me and trust Me. Tell all the ones who are even a little bit afraid to go home."

So Gideon did as God told him and about half the people went home.

"But there are still too many," God said. "Take them down to the river. Those who kneel and drink will go home. Those who cup the water in their hands and drink, will fight the battle."

Gideon did what God told him. And almost all the people knelt to drink. "You," Gideon said, pointing to the people on their knees, "all of you go on home."

"But we want to fight the Midianites," they said.

"No, the Lord said you must go home. Watch the battle and see how the Lord God wins for us, despite the small numbers," Gideon said.

After the people left, Gideon counted how many remained. There were only three hundred men. They all looked at each other, knowing it was a very small number to fight a huge army like the one across the river. "God will fight for us," Gideon said. And because he talked like he knew what he was doing, because they could tell the Spirit of God was in him, the men believed Gideon.

The three hundred men picked up all the food and weapons and trumpets the others had left behind. They sharpened their spears and dreamed about the many Midianites and their camels they would kill during the coming battle.

Listening in the Night

Judges 7:9-:15

That same night the Lord came to Gideon and told him to cross the river and spy on the Midianites. Into the deep, dark night Gideon and his servant snuck toward the Midianite camp. There were thousands and thousands of them. There were many more camels than Midianites. The fields were full of camel humps and more camel humps.

God had told Gideon, "What you hear when you spy on the Midianites will help make you win."

Gideon was too curious to be afraid. "What will I hear?" he wondered.

Gideon snuck into the camp. He hid behind a tent and heard voices inside.

As he listened, one Midianite soldier said to another, "I just had the strangest dream. A loaf of bread came tumbling into our camp and turned it upside down."

"I know what that means," the other soldier said, "that is Gideon and his Israelite army. They will beat our army tomorrow because the one, true God is leading them."

"Oh, even the Midianites are scared of me because they know God is on our side," Gideon said to his servant.

Trumpets and Torches

Judges 7:16-8:21

When Gideon heard how afraid the enemy soldiers were of him, he could hardly believe his ears. "If they are this scared," he said, "then we have almost won." Gideon bowed his head and worshipped the Lord for being so good. He thanked God for already fighting half the battle in the minds of the Midianites.

Then he snuck back to the Israelite camp. He woke up his soldiers and told them what he had heard. "We have practically won already. All we have to do is attack and make as much noise as possible so they think there are many more of us than three hundred. Tonight men, you will see how great the Lord is!" All three hundred soldiers waved their spears in the air and cheered.

"Yes," Gideon said, "just like that. When I give the sign, once we are near the Midianites, cheer as loud as you can. Yell out, 'For God and for Gideon!' That will scare them!"

Gideon divided the men into three groups and sent them out to different parts of the Midianite camp. Very quietly, the men snuck into the enemy camp. All was quiet. Not even the camels knew the Israelites were there.

Then, suddenly, at Gideon's signal, all the Israelites banged pans together, clanged their shields and blew their trumpets. It made a terrific noise! The Midianites thought a mighty army had come to attack them. They woke up with a start and ran in as many directions and as fast as they could. Because all the noise came from three different directions, they did not even know which way to run. It was a mighty victory for Gideon.

Gideon and his men lit their torches and drove off every single Midianite. Only a few got away. But even those few were not safe. Gideon and his men chased these last enemy soldiers a long, long way.

"The Lord has helped us win today," Gideon told the Israelites. And all the people bowed their heads and gave thanks to God.

"I Won't be King"

Judges 8:29-:35

After Gideon led the Israelites against the Midianites and won, the people knew he was a very great leader. They wanted him to be more than a judge to them, teaching them to follow God and showing wisdom. So the Israelites begged him to be their king.

"We need a king!"

"Yes, that is why we are always forgetting about God, we have no king!"

"Gideon, you be our king. And your sons can be our princes!"

Gideon just shook his head. "No, your King is the Lord God. You can do what He says without having a king."

Still, the people wanted to show their thanks to Gideon for freeing them from the awful Midianites and all their camels. Each gave him a golden earring.

Because the people had been reminded to worship the one, true God and because they tried hard to do what God wanted, the Lord gave them forty years of peace while Gideon lived.

After he died, though, the people forgot again. They turned to the foreign gods and once again did not follow God's laws.

God sent one judge after another, but still the people refused to listen. They were very stubborn.

THE STORY OF JEPHTHAH

"Can You Say 'Shibboleth'?"

Judges 10:6-12:7

Because the Israelite people were following foreign gods instead of the one, true Lord who had rescued them from Egypt, He allowed another enemy tribe to take the Israelites prisoner.

For eighteen years God's chosen people suffered as slaves at the hands of the Ammon tribe. Finally, they remembered who had saved them in the past. They cried to God, "Oh Lord, we are so sorry for forgetting once again. Please save us!" The Lord heard His children and could not stand their misery anymore. The people wondered which man God would choose to lead them.

God's choice was a man named Jephthah. He was a brave soldier. The Spirit of the Lord came on Jephthah, just as it had on Gideon. And he was stronger than the strongest man and wiser than the eldest leader. The Spirit of God showed Jephthah what to say, where to fight and how to arrange his soldiers. Jephthah and his soldiers defeated the Ammonites.

After the battle, though, one of the other tribes of Israel asked, "Why didn't you ask our help when you fought against Ammon?"

"But I could not wait. The Lord said to fight. It was time. I asked your help, but no one came," Jephthah said. The tribe declared war on Jephthah and his tribe.

Jephthah ordered a guard to watch the river.

Whenever someone wanted to cross the river, he had to say the password, "shibboleth." If he said "sibboleth," instead of "shibboleth" then Jephthah's guards would know he was a spy. He caught many people this way and was able to keep his people safe from harm for six years.

THE HAIR CUT

A Baby Set Apart

Judges 13:1-:25

After Jephthah died, the people of Israel did as they had so many times before. They chose to ignore God's laws. God allowed the Philistine tribe to rule over the Israelites for forty years.

At that time there was a couple who wanted a baby very badly. One day the woman was alone and an angel appeared to her.

The angel stood tall and shone like sunlight. His voice was deep. He said, "Soon you will become pregnant and have a baby boy. This baby will be special, dedicated to God from the very beginning. This means he can never have his hair cut and you must not drink any wine or eat anything which goes against God's laws while you are pregnant."

The woman nodded. She felt like jumping for joy at the idea of having a baby. But when she heard the angel's next words, she became even more amazed.

"This boy will be used by God to help drive the Philistines away from the people of Israel."

The woman picked up her skirts and ran home as fast as she could. When she found her husband, she was so out of breath she could hardly talk. The woman told her husband, Manoah, the whole story. When she was finished Manoah prayed to God, "Oh Lord, please let the man of God that You sent come back again. Please let him tell us what this plan for the life of our son really is."

The Lord answered Manoah. When the angel came back, Manoah asked his question, "Please sir, what has the Lord planned for our son?"

But the angel spoke only to his wife, "I have told you what you must do. Do not drink any wine, eat healthy food and do not cut the boy's hair."

The couple offered a sacrifice and when the angel disappeared in the fire which went up toward the sky, Manoah and his wife finally knew he was an angel.

The woman did all that the angel had told her. And she did become pregnant. Almost a year later she gave birth to a baby boy.

Manoah and his wife raised him in healthy ways and never cut his hair. That was a sign that he belonged to God. They taught him to worship God and follow His laws. God blessed the boy, whose name was Samson. God had a special plan for the life of Samson.

Fighting with a Lion

Judges 14:1-:7

As Samson grew older, the Lord sent His Holy Spirit to teach Samson what was right and wrong. God's Holy Spirit also made Samson super strong whenever God wanted to teach him a special lesson.

One such time was when Samson had grown to become a young man. He was walking to a village where many Philistines lived. His girl-friend lived there. Samson thought she was very beautiful. He loved her and wanted to make her his wife.

When he told his parents that he wanted to marry her, his parents said, "But she is not from Israel. Are you sure she is the right girl? She is from the enemy tribe. You know God has special plans for you, are you absolutely sure you want to marry this girl?"

Samson was sure. He thought she was the loveliest girl he had ever seen. And he was head over heals in love with her. Samson's parents wondered if this girl was part of God's plan for Samson. God planned on helping Samson fight the Philistines. His falling in love with this girl was the first step.

Samson and his parents went to the girl's village to make all the arrangements for the wedding.

As Samson was following his parents, who were a few hours ahead of him, he walked through a field and heard a strange sound.

"What is that?" he wondered.

Then suddenly, from out of nowhere, a great, big lion came running at him. "Raaaaahh!" the lion's long teeth shone as he opened his mouth and roared.

Samson had no weapons at all. But the Spirit of the Lord came upon him so he became stronger than the strongest man. He was super strong. And when the lion was on him, Samson threw him off and killed him. That is how strong he was.

Samson could not believe what had happened. He looked down at the dead lion and knew God must have helped him in a special way. He thanked the Lord for taking care of him.

Samson Tells a Riddle

Judges 14:8-15:20

One day, soon before the wedding, Samson passed the place where he had killed the lion. There was a swarm of bees making honey. He went over to the lion and tasted the honey. It was very sweet.

When Samson arrived at his girlfriend's house, he invited the Philistine men to a party. Even though the Philistines were enemies, because he was marrying into their tribe, he wanted to get to know them.

The night of the party about thirty young men sat around fires until late at night, telling stories and drinking. Then Samson said, "Hey, I know a good riddle. Does anyone want to place a bet with me?"

"Sure, I will."

"Yes," all the men agreed. Samson bet them thirty pieces of linen and thirty changes of clothes that they would not figure out the answer to the riddle. They had to discover the answer before the seven days of parties which followed the wedding were over. The men agreed.

Samson said, "This is the riddle: Out of the eater came something to eat. And out of the strong came something sweet."

The thirty Philistines all looked at each other. "What does it mean?" they asked.

The wedding took place and four days of feasting passed. The thirty Philistines could not figure out the answer to the riddle. And they did not want to pay for all the clothes they would need to buy for Samson if they lost.

So they went to Samson's wife. "Get Samson to tell you the riddle's answer or we will burn down your father's house and kill him and you."

The girl was very scared. She begged Samson to tell her. Day after day she nagged and cried, whined and pleaded. The party was spoiled for Samson because his bride was so miserable.

Finally Samson gave in and told his bride the answer. She told the Philistines. And they told Samson.

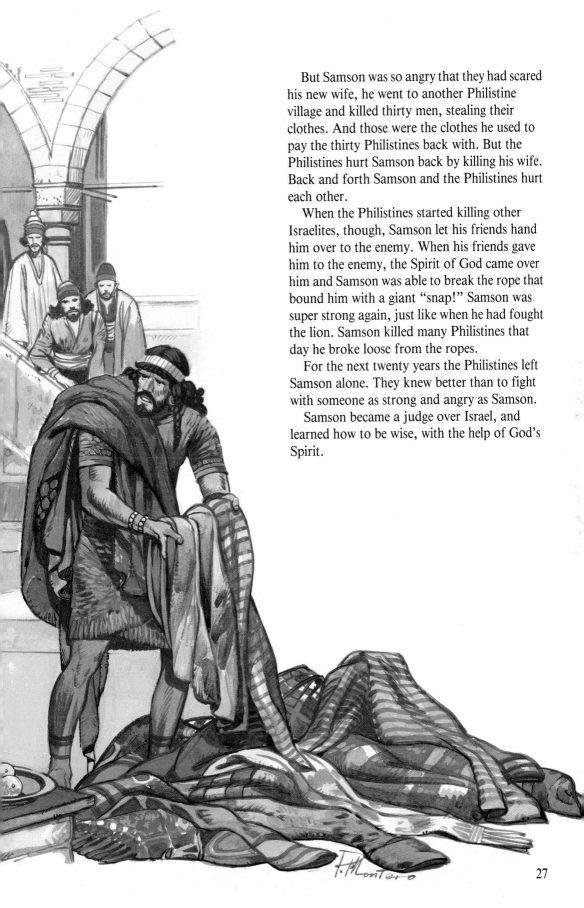

But Samson was so angry that they had scared his new wife, he went to another Philistine village and killed thirty men, stealing their clothes. And those were the clothes he used to pay the thirty Philistines back with. But the Philistines hurt Samson back by killing his wife. Back and forth Samson and the Philistines hurt each other.

When the Philistines started killing other Israelites, though, Samson let his friends hand him over to the enemy. When his friends gave him to the enemy, the Spirit of God came over him and Samson was able to break the rope that bound him with a giant "snap!" Samson was super strong again, just like when he had fought the lion. Samson killed many Philistines that day he broke loose from the ropes.

For the next twenty years the Philistines left Samson alone. They knew better than to fight with someone as strong and angry as Samson.

Samson became a judge over Israel, and learned how to be wise, with the help of God's Spirit.

Samson and Delilah

Judges 16:1-:20

While Samson judged Israel, he taught the
people how to worship God and follow His
laws. Throughout that time, the Spirit of God
helped Samson be very strong. He became
famous for his muscles. Samson could lift a
camel. With the Lord's help, Samson could do
anything.

The Philistines wanted to capture Samson,
though. They had never forgiven him for all the
destruction he had caused twenty years earlier.
They were afraid to hurt him, though, because
he was so strong.

One day, after so many years, Samson fell in
love again. The woman he loved was called
Delilah, but she was a bad woman. She made a
deal with the Philistines and agreed to trick
Samson, who had been so nice to her.

Over and over again, she nagged Samson.
"Why are you so strong? What is your secret?"

Samson would not tell. Samson did not like
being nagged. It reminded him of how he had
lost his wife. He tried to ignore Delilah. He told
her stories. "If I were tied up in wet ropes, I
would lose my strength," he said.

Delilah told the Philistines and they tied Samson up with wet ropes. It did no good. He broke free.

He said, "Tie me with new ropes and I will become weak."

The Philistines tried that, too, but once again Samson broke free.

"Braid my hair," he said, hoping Delilah would stop pestering him. "Braid my hair and I become weak like other men."

Delilah braided his hair, then called in the Philistines. But Samson was still too strong for them.

"Please, please, please, Samson. Tell me your secret!" Delilah asked Samson morning, noon and night. She would not give up. She wanted the silver pieces so badly.

Finally, Samson could not stand it any longer. "All right, woman!" he bellowed. "I've had enough! The secret of my strength is the Lord. He makes me strong as long as my hair is uncut. Ever since I was a baby my parents knew God had a plan for me."

That night Delilah called the Philistines again. She made Samson sleep on her lap and made sure he would not wake up. A man cut his hair, and when Samson woke up, it was already too late. Samson was too weak to fight the Philistines. They took Samson prisoner and paid Delilah with 1,100 pieces of silver.

29

The Strongest Man Wins

Judges 16:22-:31

When the Philistines dragged Samson away, they were very happy. After twenty years, they had captured the strong Samson, who was not so strong after all.

"All we had to do was cut your hair and now you are as weak as a baby," they teased him.

The Philistines were very mean. They hurt him so badly, Samson could not see anymore. He became blind. Then they threw him into prison. The Philistines wrapped Samson in chains and forced him to grind big rocks into gravel all day and most of the night.

Poor Samson. He was a prisoner and had no hope of escaping. But after some time his hair started to grow back again. And little by little, he felt the Lord returning his strength. He would never see again. But he prayed there might be a time when he could repay the Philistines, once and for all.

"Lord," he cried out, "give me my strength back."

With each month that Samson spent in prison he became stronger. One day, the Philistines were having a huge party in a big hall. There were over three thousand people there.

"Let's have Samson come to the party, too," they said.

"Yes, we can laugh at him."

"Silly Samson who thought he was so strong! Bring him to us," the people called.

The prison guard brought Samson to them. As Samson entered the hall, he heard the crowd and knew many of the important Philistine leaders were there. He heard them making fun of him, but all he could think was, "Lord, help me be strong."

The people ordered Samson to stand beneath two pillars. The pillars held the big house up. Samson asked the boy who was leading him to show him where the pillars were.

When Samson felt the rough stone beneath his fingers, he tossed his head back. The little bit of hair which had grown since Delilah cut it fell over his shoulders. "Lord God Almighty," he shouted. "Please give me back my strength just this once so I can hurt the Philistines. Please Lord, help me set your people free!"

And the Lord heard Samson. His Holy Spirit flooded Samson with strength and with a mighty heave, Samson pushed the pillars. He pushed and heaved and shoved and suddenly, the building shifted.

The Philistines screamed, "Earthquake!" But it was no earthquake. It was super-strong Samson, pushing the pillars out from under the building.

With a mighty crash, the stones all fell in on one another.

"Let me die with the Philistines!" Samson shouted. And he bent with all his might so that the house fell down.

31

FamilyTime Bible Stories